About Your Theme Calendar

Planned Theme Play

Young children learn through play. Planned theme play can enhance regular play by providing opportunities for children to make connections and to see relationships. It can also stimulate children's brain development by having them use multiple senses when making discoveries about a specific topic.

With planned theme play, the themes serve as fun vehicles for helping children acquire important thinking skills.

Planned theme play also helps children understand that all learning is connected—that they can learn about a topic in many different ways. For instance, they can explore the subject of caterpillars by observing a live one, by singing a caterpillar song, by making a pretend caterpillar out of modeling dough, by moving like a caterpillar, and so forth.

Learning Through Themes

When you offer young children multisensory age-appropriate activities structured around a central theme, you can be assured of early learning success.

Themes offer the opportunity to:

☆ integrate learning experiences.

☆ allow children to repeat basic skills in a variety of ways.

☆ incorporate the use of multiple senses, thus ensuring understanding, no matter what a child's dominate learning style may be.

☆ engage children and adults in quality learning time.

Your *Theme Calendar* incorporates activities that have been designed to develop the following skills.

Language skills—activities involving rhymes, stories, and puppet play.

Creative art and problem solving skills—activities that foster making choices and decisions.

Coordination skills—activities that use large and small muscles.

Music skills—activities that incorporate songs, rhymes, and rhythms—all helpful for later development of reading and math skills.

Thinking and beginning math skills—activities that deal with relationships, basic shapes, size, positions, sorting and matching, and likes and differences.

Jean Warren

Using Your Theme Calendar

☆ At the beginning of each week, look through the activities to get an overview of the contents.

☆ If a week's theme would work better for you at a different time of year, just switch weeks, substituting one for the other.

☆ Plan to do the activities spread out over the week, or do them all together, if you wish.

☆ Pick and choose the activities you think you and your child will enjoy doing.

☆ Feel free to adapt any of the activities to fit your child's age and ability, or your particular situation.

☆ As you work on an activity together, encourage conversation about what your child is doing and sensing.

☆ If your child has difficulty with an activity, don't worry. Just try another one you think is more suitable.

☆ Look for opportunities to extend the week's theme by including your own and your child's experiences that relate to the topic.

☆ Remember that having fun promotes the best learning. And working with themes keeps learning fun!

A Word About Safe activities in this boo ate for children ages it is important that a vise the activities to children do not put a objects in their mout materials, such as scis felt tip markers, use th specifically labeled as dren unless the materi used only by an adult.

January

Happy New Year

Sung to: "Frère Jacques"

So long, old year.
So long, old year.
1999. 1999.
Hello to the new year,
Hello to the new year,
2000. 2000.

Substitute the years you are observing for *1999* and *2000*.

Gayle Bittinger

Noisemaker

Help your child make a Noisemaker to ring in the new year. Place one or two small scoops of rice, dried peas, or popcorn kernels into a disposable aluminum pie pan. Cover with another pie pan and staple the edges together. Let your child shake the Noisemaker tambourine style or strike it with his hands.

New Year Parade

Make a Noisemaker for each member of your family. March around your home as you sing "Happy New Year." Let each person take turns leading the parade.

Party Menu

Let your child help you plan a menu for one of your New Year's Day meals. You could look through old favorite recipes, or browse through a cookbook to find something new to prepare together. Let him draw or write a menu to share with the other "party guests."

New Year's Crunch

Set out several kinds of cereal, a measuring cup, and a large bowl. Have your child measure 1 cup of each kind of cereal into the bowl. Let him gently mix up the cereal and put it into resealable bags. Have him serve his New Year's Crunch as a snack on New Year's Day.

Midnight Game

Tell your child he'll be listening for "midnight" when you play this game. Have him listen carefully and count as you make a bell ring. If he hears 12 rings (which means it's midnight), have him "cheer" in the new year. If he hears a different number of rings, have him stay quiet. Take turns being the "ringer."

Special Days

Look through the new year's calendar together. Let your child put stickers on special days throughout the year. Talk about what makes each of those days special.

Top It Off

Let your child help you prepare a batch of popcorn. Instead of adding the usual butter and salt, though, have some other toppings available, such as garlic salt, grated Parmesan cheese, cinnamon sugar, or shredded Cheddar cheese. Have your child select a new topping to put on her popcorn.

Measuring Game

Fill a large container partway with popcorn kernels. Add a set of measuring cups. Let your child use the kernels and cups to help her explore measuring concepts. Have her measure out 1 cup of kernels. How many quarter cups will that fill? How many third cups does it take to fill a whole cup? Continue with other measurement problems.

Sprouting Kernel

Moisten a paper towel, fold it, and put it in a resealable bag. Let your child add two or three popcorn kernels to the bag. Seal the bag shut and put it in a sunny window. Have your child check on the kernels each day. Before too long, the kernels will sprout.

Snowy Pictures

Set out a bowl of popped popcorn, a bowl with a small amount of glue in it, and some construction paper. Show your child how to dip the popcorn into the glue and then stick it onto the paper. Encourage her to make a snowy design with the popcorn.

Popcorn Guessing

Give your child a handful of popcorn to hold. Have her guess how many pieces of popcorn are in her hand. Count the popcorn together. Was her guess too high or too low? Try again. The more times she does this, the better she will become at guessing.

For the Birds

Poke two holes at the top of a cardboard tube and tie on a loop of yarn. Help your child spread peanut butter all over the outside of the tube, and then roll the tube in popped popcorn. Hang the popcorn feeder outside for all the birds to enjoy.

Pop! Pop! Pop!

Sung to: "Row, Row, Row Your Boat"

Pop, pop, pop, pop, pop!

Popcorn in a pot.

I love to eat it every day.

I hope it never stops.

Sing this song while waiting for your popcorn to pop.

Jean Warren

January

Peace Art

Cut a simple dove shape out of construction paper. Help your child brush glue all over the dove and decorate it with ribbon, yarn, and fancy paper. Let him sprinkle on some glitter when he is finished.

Positive Statements

Brainstorm a list of "Good Feeling Statements" with your child. Examples might include "Thanks for helping me" or "I'm glad you're in my family." Write these statements on a sheet of paper and hang them up where your child can see them.

Martin Luther King Day

The third Monday of January is Martin Luther King Day. Talk about the life and triumphs of Dr. Martin Luther King Jr. with your child. Go to the library and check out a book about him. Help your child think of ways to be kind and peaceful toward others.

Peace Cake

Let your child help you make this cake to share with others. Open up two cans of refrigerated biscuits and separate the biscuits. Divide each biscuit into quarters. Dip the quarters into melted butter and roll them in cinnamon sugar. Put the quarters in a bundt cake pan. Bake at 350°F for 30–35 minutes. Turn out of the pan onto a serving plate and cool.

Friendship Collage

Help your child cut out magazine pictures of all different kinds of people. Let him glue the pictures onto a large sheet of paper to make a Friendship Collage. Talk about what a friend is. Ask questions: Can you be a friend with someone who looks different from you? Who is older or younger than you? Who likes different things than you do?

Peace Wreath

Draw a large wreath shape on a large sheet of heavy-duty gift-wrap. Hang up the wrapping paper in a prominent place. Help your child trace around his hands on construction paper and cut out the shapes. Have him tape the hands on the circle on the paper. Encourage him to have each person who visits your home make paper handprints to add to the wreath.

We Know How to Get Along

Sung to: "Mary Had a Little Lamb"

We know how to get along,
Get along, get along.
We know how to get along
Every single day!

We take turns and share a lot,
Share a lot, share a lot.
We take turns and share a lot
While we work and play!

Sing while your child plays peacefully with another child.

Kathy McCullough

Count It Up

Sung to: "London Bridge"

Here's my money, count it up,

Count it up, count it up.

Here's my money, count it up,

Count it up today.

Set out coins for your child to count while you sing this song.

Gayle Bittinger

The Change Game

Set out a small pile of coins and let your child sort it. She can put each kind of coin in a separate container. When she is finished, help her count each pile of coins.

Piggy Bank

Select a container with a lid (a yogurt container, a round oatmeal box, or a shoebox). Let your child decorate the box with stickers, crayons, or felt tip markers. Give your child a few coins to put in her completed Piggy Bank. You may wish to let her sort through your coins each day and select all the pennies (or other coin you choose) to put in her bank.

Play Money

Help your child cut recycled paper into small rectangles. She can write numbers on the rectangles to designate different denominations. You can also cut circles out of heavy paper for coins. Your child will love to play with the money she creates.

I'll Buy That

Set up a "store" with your child. Let her arrange several items, such as toys or canned goods, on a shelf and tell you when her store is open. Pretend to be a customer looking at the items and selecting some to purchase. Then switch places. You may want to add a shopping basket and some shopping bags.

Coin Rubbings

Tape several coins to a flat surface. Show your child how to place a sheet of paper over the coins and rub the flat side of an unwrapped crayon over them. Let her make several different rubbings. You can also cut these rubbings out to make "coins."

Cash Register

Make a register till for your child to use while sorting and playing "store." Find a plastic container with several divided sections, such as a utensil tray or a desk organizer, or collect several small boxes and tape them together. Let your child arrange the money in her "till" just as she wants.

February

Open, Close

Open, close. Open, close,

Make the scissors go.

Open, close. Open, close,

Cut the paper so.

Recite the rhyme as your child uses his scissors to cut paper.

Gayle Bittinger

Triangle Snips

Cut large triangles out of construction paper. Show your child how to snip off the corners to make smaller triangles. Let him see how many small triangles he can cut from one large triangle.

Cutting Circles

Cut 2-inch squares out of construction paper. Have your child watch as you use the scissors to round the corners of one of the squares to make a circle. Let your child try cutting out a circle or two.

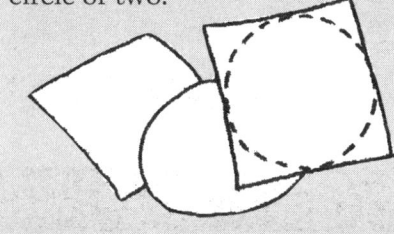

Basket Strips

Draw lines about ¼ inch apart on a sheet of construction paper. Have your child cut along the lines to make thin strips. Let him weave the strips in and out of a plastic berry basket.

Garland Cutting

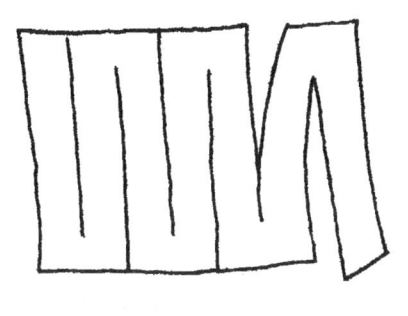

Show your child how to turn an ordinary sheet of paper into a fancy garland. Draw lines on a sheet of paper as shown in the illustration. Have your child cut on the lines. Gently pull the paper apart to make the garland. Let your child make as many garlands as he would like. Use the garlands to decorate the room.

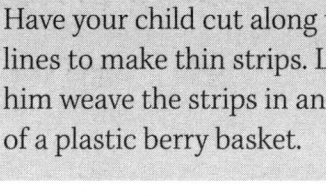

Straw Collage

Collect several drinking straws. Let your child cut them into 1- to 2-inch lengths. When he is finished, let him glue the pieces onto a piece of construction paper to make a Straw Collage.

Fruit Cutups

Thoroughly wash a pair of scissors to use in food preparation. Let your child use the scissors to cut up sections of fruit, such as apple slices, orange wedges, bananas, cantaloupe wedges, and strawberry halves. Mix the fruit together, serve, and enjoy.

Hunting for Hearts

Cut heart shapes out of construction paper. Hide the hearts around a room in your home. Let your child hunt for the hearts. When she has found all of them, let her hide them for you to find.

Candy Heart Fun

Put some candy hearts on a tray. Let your child sort them by color. Encourage her to use the hearts to make patterns. Read the words on the hearts together.

Heart Waffles

Toast frozen waffles and let your child use a cookie cutter to cut them into heart shapes. Have her decorate the hearts by sprinkling on powdered sugar. Enjoy.

Love Book

Encourage your child to think of things and people she loves. Cut several large heart shapes out of construction paper. Stack them on top of one another and staple them together on one side. Write "I Love ..." on the cover. Let your child draw pictures of her favorite things and people on the inside pages.

Red Pineapple Punch

Mix together 1 can (46 ounces) pineapple juice, 6 cups cold water, and 1 packet unsweetened tropical punch soft-drink mix. Stir well. Chill. Let your child serve her special punch at lunch or dinner.

Heart Baskets

Help your child cut heart shapes out of the bottom corners of old envelopes (see illustration). Give her thin strips of construction paper to tape on for handles. Let her fill the hearts with candy and deliver them to friends and family.

On Valentine's Day

Sung to: "Bingo"

On Valentine's Day,

A special day,

I give each friend a heart.

H-E-A-R-T,

H-E-A-R-T,

H-E-A-R-T,

I give each friend a heart.

Write the letters H-E-A-R-T on a heart shape to make it easier for your child to follow along while singing this song.

Susan A. Miller

February

Counting Hearts

Have your child spread out all of his Valentine's Day cards on the table and count them. Take some of the cards away. Have him count the ones that are left. Rearrange the cards and have him count them again. If he likes, help him count his cards by twos.

Number Walk

Number 20 index cards from 1 to 20. Arrange them in a path leading from one room to another, but make sure the numbers are not in order. Put a small treat by the last card. Have your child start at the beginning of the path, picking up one card at a time and saying the number on it.

Dot to Dot

With your child, make dot-to-dot puzzles for each other. Use felt tip markers to make dots on sheets of paper, then use a pencil to number the dots, starting at number one. Complete each other's dot-to-dots. Compare your pictures. Which one is the silliest?

Number Book

Cut ten sheets of paper in half. Staple the 20 half sheets together to make a book. Help your child number the pages from 1 to 20. Let him draw the appropriate number of items on each page, or let him make rubber stamp designs or put on stickers. "Read" his Number Book together.

Number Pokey

Write numbers on plain colored stickers. Put the stickers on you and your child. Sing the "Hokey-Pokey," substituting numbers for the names of body parts. For example, "You put your number 5 in, you put your number 5 out. You put your number 5 in and you shake it all about." Continue until you have sung about all of the numbers.

One-Cup Salad

Let your child help you cut a variety of fresh vegetables into bite-size pieces. Have him measure out 1 cup of each of the vegetables and put them together in a large bowl. Pour on some salad dressing, stir gently, and serve.

Start at Number One

Sung to: "The Farmer in the Dell"

Counting is such fun.

We start at number one.

We count and count

Until we're done.

Counting is such fun.

Each time you sing this song with your child, pick something else to count.

Gayle Bittinger

Brush Your Teeth

Sung to: "If You're Happy and You Know It"

When you want to
Brush your teeth—
Wiggle-jiggle.
When you want to
Brush your teeth—
Wiggle-jiggle.
First you wiggle,
Then you jiggle.
Brush your tongue
Until you giggle.
When you want to
Brush your teeth—
Wiggle-jiggle.

Sing this song while your child brushes her teeth.

Gayle Bittinger

Seeing the Dentist

Role-play a dentist visit with your child. Have your child pretend to be the patient while you "check" her teeth and brush them. Then let your child pretend to be the dentist while you are the patient. This kind of practice makes a real visit to the dentist less worrisome for your child.

Smiling Picture

Cut a large lips shape out of red construction paper. Cut a thin strip of white paper. Let your child snip the white paper strip into little pieces to make "teeth." Have her glue her teeth on her lips shape to make a big toothy grin.

Brushing Chart

Make a brushing chart to hang up in the bathroom. Each time your child brushes her teeth, have her put an *X* next to the appropriate day. If she has at least two *X*'s by each day for a week, let her pick out a small treat such as some new stickers or a trip to the park.

Brushing Time

One of the most important parts of tooth brushing for a young child is getting her to brush long enough. Help your child do this by setting a timer for two minutes (or the time suggested by your dentist).

Happy Tooth

Draw happy faces on ten circle stickers. Talk with your child about the kinds of food you can eat to help your teeth stay healthy and strong. Let her help you look in your kitchen to find ten healthy foods that would make her teeth happy. Let her put a sticker on each of the healthy foods.

Nature's Toothbrush

It is said that an apple is nature's "toothbrush." Give your child an apple slice or two to eat after a meal. Do her teeth feel cleaner?

March

Is the Sun Out?

Sung to: "Frère Jacques"

What's the weather?

What's the weather?

Do you know?

Do you know?

Is the sun out?

Is the sun out?

What's the weather?

What's the weather?

Substitute other kinds of weather for *Is the sun out?*

Gayle Bittinger

Stormy Weather

Play a nature tape with storm sounds. Let your child adjust the volume to make the storm as loud or as quiet as he likes.

Wind Watching

Hang some ready-made windsocks and wind chimes outside a window. Let your child watch and listen when the wind blows. What does he see? What does he hear?

Weather Clothes

Set out two pieces of construction paper. Have your child draw a sun on one paper and a snowflake on the other. Let him cut out magazine pictures of people dressed for warm weather and people dressed for cold weather. Have him glue the pictures on the page with the appropriate weather.

Weather Calendar

Find a calendar with large squares. Each day, look outside with your child and observe the weather. Let your child draw a picture of the weather he sees (sun, raindrops, clouds, snowflakes, etc.) in the appropriate calendar square. If you wish, hang a thermometer outside and observe and record the temperature as well.

Cloud Art

Give your child a piece of light blue construction paper. Have him fold the paper in half and unfold it. Let him use an eyedropper to squeeze three or four drops of white tempera paint on one side of the paper. Have him refold the paper and rub across it with his hand. Let him open his paper to reveal his cloud picture. Let him make more Cloud Art as he wishes.

Rain Watching

Make a rain gauge with your child by using a permanent felt tip marker to mark inch measurements on the side of a clear-plastic jar. Let your child place the jar outside in a secure place. Each day, check the jar for rainfall. If you wish, have your child record the amount of rainfall on his Weather Calendar.

Potato Prints

Cut a large potato shape out of a brown paper bag. Cut real potatoes into various small shapes. Let your child dip the real potato shapes into paint and use them to print designs on the paper potato shape.

Sweet Potato Plants

Help your child insert three or four toothpicks horizontally around the middle of a sweet potato. Fill a glass with water. Show your child how to balance the toothpicks on the rim of the glass so that one end of the potato is in the water. Have her check on the water level each day, adding more as needed. In about two weeks, the potato will begin to sprout.

Potato Patterns

Buy two different kinds of potatoes at the grocery store. Wash them and set them out on the table. Encourage your child to sort the potatoes, then use them to make different patterns, such as russet-russet-red-russet-russet-red or white-red-white-red-white-red.

Potato Hop

Try this challenging game with your child. Hold a potato between your knees. Count how many times you can hop up and down before you drop the potato. Try to hold the potato longer each time.

Mashed Potatoes

Cut washed unpeeled potatoes into cubes about $1/4$ inch thick. Steam them in a steamer or an electric skillet for 3 minutes or until tender. When the potatoes have cooled slightly, add a little milk or broth and let your child help you mash them. Sing the "Mash, Mash" song while you mash them. Serve the potatoes with butter, if desired.

Hot Potato

Collect a ball and a timer. Set the timer for one or two minutes. Toss the "hot potato" (the ball) back and forth with your child. Whoever is holding the ball when the timer goes off gets to set the timer for the next round.

Mash, Mash

Sung to: "Skip to My Lou"

Mash, mash,

Mash potatoes.

Mash, mash,

Mash potatoes.

Mash, mash,

Mash potatoes,

Mash them up for me.

Mash potatoes while you sing this song.

Gayle Bittinger

March

Golden Thoughts

Cut a large pot-of-gold shape out of black paper. Hang it up in a prominent place. Cut circles out of yellow construction paper for gold pieces. Talk with your child about golden thoughts, or thoughts that are kind and loving. Ask your child to think of golden thoughts to write on the paper gold pieces. Let him tape the gold pieces to the top of the pot-of-gold shape.

Treasure Hunt

Tie a piece of yarn to your child's bed while he is sleeping the night before St. Patrick's Day. Wind the yarn all over the house, tying a "pot of gold" (or other treasure) to the end of it. When your child awakens, have him follow the yarn to discover his treasure.

St. Patty's Day Story

Place several green items in a large bag. If possible, include a few St. Patrick's Day items such as a shamrock, a leprechaun hat, or a pretend pot of gold. Begin a story about you and your child on St. Patrick's Day. Pull an item out of the bag and incorporate it into the story. Then let your child take out an item and continue the story himself. Take turns with your child, pulling out the items and incorporating them into your story.

Heart Shamrocks

Show your child how to make a shamrock out of heart shapes. Cut three heart shapes out of green paper. Arrange them on a sheet of paper with their points touching. Let your child glue them in a place and add a green stem. Let him make as many Heart Shamrocks as he would like.

Gold Hunt

Hide objects around the room that are the color of gold, such as jewelry, keys, pens, and hair clips. Set out a large black pot. Let your child "help the leprechaun fill his pot with gold" by searching for the hidden gold-colored objects and placing them in the pot. When all of the objects have been found, let your child count them.

Surprise Pudding

Spoon ready-made vanilla pudding into a small bowl. Add a drop of blue food coloring and a drop of yellow food coloring. Have your child stir his pudding with a spoon and watch what happens.

It's St. Patrick's Day

Sung to: "Mary Had a Little Lamb"

Leprechauns and

Shamrocks green,

Shamrocks green,

Shamrocks green.

Leprechauns and

Shamrocks green,

It's St. Patrick's Day.

Wear green shamrock shapes while you sing this song.

Carla C. Skjong

Spring

Sung to: "The Farmer in the Dell"

Spring is finally here.

Winter days are past.

Little flowers raise their heads,

Snow is gone at last!

See the trees in green,

Dressed up just for spring.

See the robins fly about,

Listen to them sing!

Sing this song while you go on a spring hike with your child.

Susan M. Paprocki

Spring Picnic

Pack up a picnic snack and take it outside to eat with your child. Let her find some blooming flowers or a budding tree to sit by. What other signs of spring can she find?

Spring Rhyme

Let your child pretend to be a flower seed curled up and waiting for spring. Have her listen while you say lots of words. As soon as she hears a word that rhymes with *spring*, such as *ring* or *thing*, have her start "growing." Play the game again, this time with you as the flower seed and your child as the "rhymer."

Spring Treat

Spring is a great time for fresh green vegetables. Let your child help you prepare a variety of vegetables and some vegetable dip. Sit down with your child and enjoy the veggies and dip together.

Spring Birds

Many birds are busy building nests in the spring. Show your child one way to help them by collecting bits of bright-colored yarn and fabric scraps. Put the yarn and fabric in a mesh bag and hang it on a nearby tree. Let your child look out the window and watch for any birds that come by to take some of the yarn or fabric. Walk around your neighborhood to look for the nests of the birds that used your special materials.

Spring Planting

Take a trip to a local nursery to look at all of the plants. Designate a planter or section of yard that your child can use to plant her own garden. On a sheet of paper, help her draw an outline of her garden space and let her plan what she would like to plant there. Encourage her to remember her favorite plants from the nursery.

Spring Blossoms

Draw a simple bare tree outline on a sheet of paper. Let your child use crayons, paints, or felt tip markers to add blossoms to the tree. Hang up her blossom-covered tree to remind your family that spring weather is coming soon. Watch for trees in your area as they begin to blossom.

April

I Saw a Sight Today

Sung to: "Row, Row, Row Your Boat"

I saw a sight today

While on my way to school.

I saw a bee with a shoe on its knee.

Surprise—it's April Fools'!

With your child, make up new third lines like these: *I saw a bear who was combing its hair; I saw a cat who was wearing a hat; I saw a fish with a serving dish.*

Elizabeth McKinnon

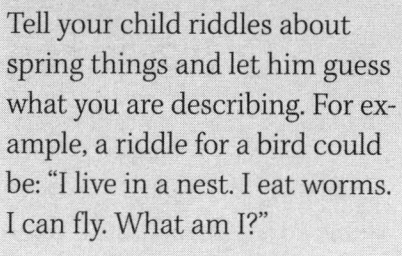

True or False

Play this listening game with your child. Say a sentence out loud. If it is true, have your child do nothing. If it is false, have your child tickle you. Take turns saying true and false sentences.

Upside Down and Backward

While your child is asleep, rearrange a room in your home by turning things upside down and backward—pictures, books, chairs, tables, and toys. Let your child name all the things that are different as you put them back to their original condition. If you wish, let him rearrange things for you to discover.

Riddles

Tell your child riddles about spring things and let him guess what you are describing. For example, a riddle for a bird could be: "I live in a nest. I eat worms. I can fly. What am I?"

Biscuit Suprises

Open a can of refrigerated biscuits. Separate a biscuit into two halves and put on a small spoonful of jam. Put the halves back together. Repeat for each biscuit. Bake according to package directions. Allow the biscuits to cool. Let your child bite into one of the biscuits to discover the surprise inside.

Water Magic

Place one or two items that float, such as a cork or a small plastic toy, in a sink full of water. Show your child how to make the items sink by placing a clear-plastic cup over them and pushing the cup straight down into the water. It looks like magic. Let your child try sinking the items.

Tops and Bottoms

Cut out pictures of people and animals from magazines. Cut each picture in half to make one "top" and one "bottom." Put all the tops in one pile and all the bottoms in another. Give your child construction paper and glue. Let him choose tops and bottoms to put together to create his own funny creatures.

Easter Egg Treasure Hunt

On slips of paper, write simple clues for a treasure hunt such as "Look by the tree that's as tall as me" or "Look under your bed by a sock that is red." Number the clues. As you set them out to make the treasure hunt, slip each clue inside a plastic egg before hiding it. Fill a large plastic egg with Easter treats for the treasure.

Egg Roll

Fill plastic eggs with different materials such as toothpicks, pebbles, salt, and dried beans. Tape the eggs closed. Ask your child to guess which eggs will roll the farthest when given a strong push. Then let her experiment to find out.

Egg Toss

Set out a large basket or box. Take turns with your child tossing plastic eggs into it. Make the game harder by tossing the eggs from farther away, with your eyes closed, with your back to the basket, and so on.

Grassy Baskets

Start this project about ten days before Easter. Let your child spoon potting soil into an old Easter basket. Have her sprinkle on grass seeds and water. Place the basket in a sunny spot and let her water the soil when it is dry. By Easter, the basket should be filled with real grass.

Spin the Eggs

Let your child examine two eggs in their shells, one uncooked and one hard-cooked. Can she tell which is which by just looking at them? Show her how to tell the difference by standing them on end and spinning them. The uncooked egg, with liquid inside, wobbles and falls down. The hard-cooked egg, which is solid inside, spins like a top. Help her crack open the eggs to confirm her guesses.

Egg-cellent Sandwiches

Cut slices of bread into oval egg shapes and spread them with peanut butter. Let your child decorate the egg-shaped sandwiches with shredded carrots, banana slices, and raisins.

Easter's Here

Sung to: "Twinkle, Twinkle, Little Star"

Easter, Easter, Easter's here.

Bunnies, chickies, let us cheer!

Easter Bunny hops with joy,

Eggs for every girl and boy.

Easter, Easter, Easter's here.

Bunnies, chickies, let us cheer!

Sing while you and your child hop like bunnies.

Ingrid Skjong

April

Patterns All Around

Encourage your child to notice the patterns all around him: the pattern of red and white stripes on the American flag, the blue and green stripe pattern on his shirt, or a colorful pattern on a sheet of gift-wrap. Help him name the patterns.

Nature Patterns

Go outside with your child and look for patterns. Can he find a pattern on a leaf or a flower? Collect some rocks and twigs and make patterns together. Try two-part patterns like rock-twig-rock-twig and three-part patterns like small rock–big rock–twig–small rock–big rock–twig.

Necklace Patterns

Collect large plastic beads in various colors or a variety of pasta shapes with holes (macaroni, rigatoni, pasta wheels), and some yarn. Help your child decide on a pattern. Let him string the beads or pasta on the yarn in that pattern to make a necklace.

Sound Patterns

Collect two each of the following items: metal pan lid, plastic container, glass bowl, and metal spoon. Divide up the items so you and your child each have one complete set. Sit with your backs to each other. Start by banging on the lid, container, and bowl in a pattern. Have your child listen carefully to the pattern and then repeat it with his own items. Then let him make up a pattern for you to copy.

Toy Patterns

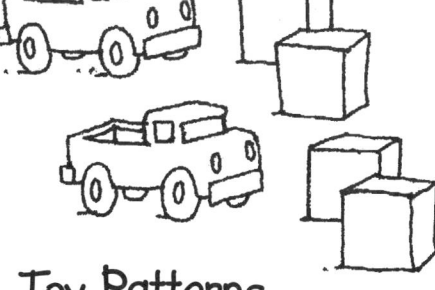

Select two toys that you have many of, such as toy blocks and toy cars. Make a pattern with the blocks and cars. Have your child repeat the pattern and then continue it.

Kabob Patterns

Let your child help you prepare a variety of fruits for kabobs. For example, you could cut bananas, cantaloupe, and watermelon into chunks, stem strawberries, and peel oranges and divide them into segments. Set out the fruit and some bamboo skewers. Put the fruit on the skewers in patterns. Try to think of a different pattern for each skewer.

Clap-Tap-Snap

Sung to: "Three Blind Mice"

Clap, tap, snap.

Clap, tap, snap.

Tap, tap, clap.

Tap, tap, clap.

I clap and snap and clap and snap.

I tap and clap and tap and clap.

I make a pattern with clap, tap, snap.

Oh, clap, tap, snap.

Make the sounds as you sing the words. Let your child make up his own clap-tap-snap patterns.

Gayle Bittinger

What Will You See?

Sung to: "Row, Row, Row Your Boat"

Look, look in a mirror,
What do you see?
You see yourself, yes, you do,
Reflected perfectly.

Look, look in a mirror,
What do you see?
A waving hand, a smiling face,
Reflected perfectly.

Have your child look in a mirror while you sing this song.

Gayle Bittinger

Dress-Up Fun

Put out dress-up clothes in front of a full-length mirror. Let your child try on the clothes and look at her reflection in the mirror.

Mirror Hunt

Take your child on a hunt for mirrors in your home. Look for a handheld mirror, a pocket mirror, a mirror that hangs on a wall, a bicycle mirror, even a mirror on a car. Let your child explore the mirrors. What does she see when she looks into each mirror? Her reflection! Ask her to describe the different mirrors. How are they alike? How are they different?

Reflection Art

Cut out magazine pictures of familiar objects that are symmetrical, such as a pair of glasses, a face, a slice of bread, or a plate. Cut those pictures in half. Show your child how to hold a rectangular mirror beside one of the pictures so that it looks whole again.

Spoon Mirror

Help your child look at her reflection on the back of a spoon. What happens when she moves the spoon back and forth and up and down? Her reflection changes from thin to wide. Now have her look into the front of her spoon. Her reflection is upside down.

Mirror Me

Stand facing your child. Have your child pretend to be a mirror and imitate all your movements. Be sure to move slowly at first. After a while, trade places and let your child make the movements while you pretend to be the mirror and imitate them.

Reflection Hunt

Talk with your child about her reflection that she saw in all of the mirrors. Are there any other things she sees her reflection in? Look around your home for objects you can see a reflection in. Collect as many of these as possible. Look at the objects together to discover what they all have in common. (All of the objects are smooth and shiny.)

May

I Made a May Basket

Sung to: "A-Tisket, A-Tasket"

A-tisket, a-tasket,

I made a May basket.

I filled it up with flowers bright

And hung it on the door just right.

Pretend to hang May baskets on door handles while you sing this song.

Jean Warren

Envelope May Baskets

Seal a long envelope and cut it in half crosswise. Turn each half into a "basket" by taping on a ribbon handle. Let your child decorate the baskets with crayons or markers. Then have him fill the baskets with real or paper flowers to give on May Day.

Flower Jar

Let your child place a small amount of clay in the lid of a baby food jar. Have him arrange a few dried flowers in the clay. Help him screw the jar onto the lid upside down and tie a ribbon around the neck to complete the Flower Jar.

Window Flowers

Let your child help you grate old crayons that have the papers removed. Have him arrange the shavings between two sheets of waxed paper. While your child watches, cover the waxed paper with a damp cloth and move a warm iron across the cloth to melt the crayons. (Only an adult should touch the iron.) When the waxed paper has cooled, let your child cut out flower shapes to hang in a window.

Flower Science

Let your child help you select a flower to study. Help him name the different parts of the flower such as the stem, leaves, and petals. Look at the different parts of the flower with a magnifying glass. What do they look like now?

Estimating Game

Find a flower with many petals. Ask your child to guess how many petals the flower has. Together, pull off the petals and count them. Was his guess too high or too low or exactly right? Repeat with more of the same kind of flower and with different kinds of flowers.

Egg Flower Snack

Hard-cook several eggs and allow them to cool. Slice the eggs into thin rounds. Let your child help you arrange the egg slices on plates to look like flowers, with one egg slice in the middle and several egg-slice "petals" around it. Add celery "stems" and lettuce "leaves," if you wish.

Gardening in Rows

Remove the lid from an egg carton and cut the bottom in half lenghtwise so you are left with two rows of six egg cups each. Let your child spoon some potting soil into each egg cup and plant one or two fast-growing seeds, such as radish seeds and marigold seeds. Have her water her rows of "garden." Encourage her to check on her seeds each day and water them as needed.

Seed Experiment

Find a clear-plastic container with a snap-on lid. Have your child fill the container with pea or bean seeds. Pour in water to the top of the container and put on the lid. Over the course of six to eight hours, the seeds absorb the water, swell, and pop the top off the container.

Silly Shoe Planter

Let your child select one of her old outgrown shoes or maybe even one of your no-longer-worn shoes for a planter. Help her fill the shoe with soil and add seeds or small plants. Place the Silly Shoe Planter on a tray to catch spills when watering.

Pizza Herb Garden

Let your child help you select two "pizza herbs," such as basil and oregano, to grow. Purchase the plants at a nursery and place them in a sunny window at home. Let your child help you pinch off some of the leaves for you to chop up and put in tomato sauce. Top toasted English muffins with the sauce and some mozzarella cheese. Broil until cheese melts.

Sprout Pet

Trace an animal shape on a sponge and cut it out (tracing around cookie cutters makes this easy). Have your child place her shape on a plate and carefully pour on enough water to saturate the sponge and leave a small amount of water pooling on the plate. Let her sprinkle alfalfa seeds on her shape. Place the shape in a warm area, and in a few days your child's "pet" will begin to sprout green "hair."

Garden Snack

Take your child to a vegetable stand or farmer's market and let her pick out one or two vegetables to try. Prepare the vegetables and share them with your child while you enjoy the view of a garden at your home or in a nearby park.

A Seed

Sung to: "This Old Man"

Plant a seed.

Water it right.

Let the sun shine,

Oh, so bright.

Then we'll watch a seed grow,

One-two-three.

It's as easy as can be.

Sing this song as your child plants and cares for her seeds.

Angela Wolfe-Batten

May

Cross the Street

Show your child how to cross a street safely: Stop at the side of the road and look and listen for traffic. When he sees and hears no cars, trucks, or other vehicles, it is safe to cross quickly and carefully. Do this with your child each time you cross the street together.

Stoplight Game

Talk with your child about what each color on a stoplight means, then play this game with him. When you say, "Green," have your child move around the room quickly. When you say, "Yellow," have him slow down. When you say, "Red," have him stop wherever he is. Repeat. Let your child have a chance to say the colors while you move around the room.

Bicycle Safety Game

Whenever you and your child are out together, look at all the bicyclists. Encourage your child to tell you what they are doing that is safe and what they are doing that is not safe.

Fire Drill

Planning and practicing a fire drill is very important. Let your child help you find at least two ways out of his room. Talk about what he would do if he heard the smoke alarm in your home, then practice it. Emphasize the importance of getting out of the home. Go over your family's fire drill a few times each year.

Stop, Drop, and Roll

Talk with your child about how to "stop, drop, and roll" if his clothes catch on fire. Clear a large area in a room or go outside to a grassy area. At a given signal, have him stop what he is doing, drop to the floor or the ground and cover his face, and roll over and over until the pretend flames are out.

Call 9-1-1

Let your child practice dialing 9-1-1 on a play phone. Pretend to be the 9-1-1 dispatcher and ask him questions such as "What happened? What is your name? What is your address?" Talk about appropriate times for calling 9-1-1, such as when someone is seriously hurt or he sees a fire or an accident.

The Number to Call

Sung to: "Mary Had a Little Lamb"

9-1-1 is the number to call,

Number to call, number to call.

9-1-1 is the number to call

When you need some help.

Sing this song often to help your child remember the 911 emergency number.

Brenda Sites

Shining My Shoes

Sung to: "Pop! Goes the Weasel"

I spread some polish on my shoes,

Then I let it dry.

I brush and brush and brush and
  brush.

Look! My shoes shine.

Have your child pretend to shine shoes
as you sing.

Adapted Traditional

Shoe Art

Help your child trace around her
shoe on a sheet of construction
paper. Have your child use crayons or felt tip markers to turn
her shoe tracing into a funny
picture. Repeat with as many
different shoe tracings as your
child wishes.

Shoe Talk

Collect five or six kinds of shoes
that people wear to do different
activities. Some examples would
be sandals, rubber boots, hiking
boots, tennis shoes, and slippers.
Show the shoes to your child and
have her describe what a person
wearing them might be doing.

Listening Game

Show your child several pairs of
shoes, such as tennis shoes, high
heels, rubber boots, and slippers,
that make different sounds
when walked across a tile floor
or a tabletop. Have your child
close her eyes as you "walk" one
of the pairs of shoes across the
floor or tabletop. Let her guess
which pair it was. Repeat with
the remaining shoes.

Glitter Shoes

Help your child decorate an old
pair of shoes with glitter. Let her
wear the shoes for special occa-
sions. (You may wish to have her
wear the shoes outside only, as
the glitter does flake off.)

Shoe Lacing

Find a sturdy boot or tennis
shoe with big eyelets. Give your
child a shoelace and show her
how to lace up the boot or shoe
to make a crisscross pattern.
Take out the shoelace and let
her think of another way to lace
up the shoe.

Shine Those Shoes

Let your child help you shine
a pair of shoes. Once she has
selected a pair of shoes that
need polishing, have her find
polish to match. Show her how
to rub the polish all over the
leather and allow it to dry. When
the shoes are ready, let her buff
them until the leather shines.

June

One-Two-Three

Sung to: "Mary Had a Little Lamb"

Right on target, one-two-three,

Look at me, one-two-three.

Right on target, one-two-three,

Ready, now watch me.

Sing as your child tosses a beanbag at a target.

Gayle Bittinger

Toss It

Collect several beanbags, rolled-up socks, or resealable plastic bags filled with dried beans (seal in two bags to minimize leakage). Let your child toss the beanbags into a box or basket. Move the target farther away or in different places around the room (on the couch, under the table, down the hall, etc.) to make the game easier or more challenging.

Clown Face

Draw a simple clown face on a large sheet of cardboard. Cut out the mouth shape. Lean the cardboard against a chair. Put down a masking-tape line about 5 feet from the clown. Let your child try tossing beanbags into the clown's mouth. Move the line closer or farther away, depending on his ability.

Flashlight Aim

Collect flashlights for your child and yourself. Sit in a darkened room. Take turns aiming your flashlights at different objects in the room. If you wish, have a race to see who can find the most of something, such as the most green items, the most items with names that start with *A*, and so on.

Bell Toss

Hang a bell outside so that it is just out of reach. Let your child try tossing beanbags at it to make it ring. Encourage him to stand farther and farther away with each successful toss.

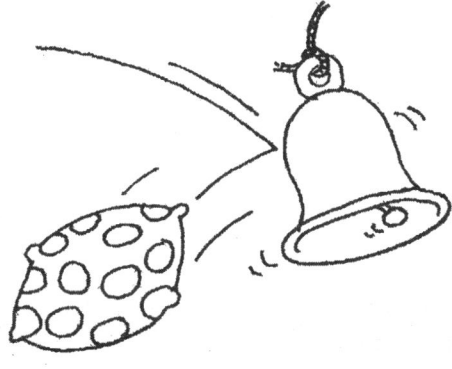

Water Target

Collect several empty plastic bottles. Add an inch or two of water to the bottom of each bottle. Set up the bottles on a fence or ledge outside. Give your child a water hose and nozzle. Turn the water on and let him aim the stream of water at the bottles to see how many he can knock over.

Toss for Snack

Set out several large pans or bowls on your kitchen floor. Put a different, sturdy kind of snack food, such as carrot sticks, a box of juice, some apple slices, or a few pretzels, in each pan. Let your child toss beanbags into the pans. If his beanbag goes into a pan, give him that snack.

Flags, Flags, Flags

Look at pictures of flags with your child. Talk with her about them. Explain that flags remind people of things that are important to them. Countries, clubs, and organizations design and display flags. What does she see when she looks at the flags? What kinds of pictures are there? Which flag is her favorite?

Design a Flag

Let your child design her own paper flag. Help her think of the colors she would like her flag to have. Have her draw pictures or symbols of important things in her life. Let her keep her flag in her room.

Flag Parade

Find small flags to wave, or use your child's flag from the Design a Flag activity. March all around your home as you sing "Marching By." Wave your flags up and down. Take turns leading the parade.

Stars and Stripes

Show your child a picture of the American flag. Have her name the color pattern that the stripes make (red-white-red-white). Count the stars together. Then let her make a Stars and Stripes Collage by gluing red and white stripes and white stars on a sheet of blue construction paper.

Flags in the Wind

Pretend with your child that you are flags hanging on flagpoles and that the wind is blowing. Together, think of ways to move in a gentle breeze, a wild storm, or a sudden calm

Cracker Flags

Put small amounts of white frosting in three bowls. Add red food coloring to one bowl and blue food coloring to another. Let your child decorate graham crackers with the red, white, and blue frosting to create "flags."

Marching By

Sung to: "When the Saints Go Marching In"

Oh, when the flags go marching by,

Oh, when the flags go marching by

How we love to see all the colors,

When the flags go marching by.

Jean Warren

June

Summer Picnic

Let your child help you pack a picnic lunch. Be sure to pack a few special summer fruits such as watermelon slices and grapes. Spread a blanket outdoors in the shade of a tree. Enjoy your picnic together. When you are finished, lie back on the blanket and watch the clouds and birds float by.

Blue Skies

Have your child use crayons to draw a summer scene on a sheet of white construction paper. Encourage him to think about all of the things he sees in the summer. When he is finished, let him paint blue watercolor all over his drawing to create "blue skies."

Summer Games

Many special athletic events happen over the summer. Have your own backyard games and invite some of your child's friends over. Try games such as the Balance on the Beam (on a 2 by 4), Jump Over the Pillows, and the Flying Disk Throw. Make medals by covering cardboard circles with foil. Give one to each child who participates.

Summer Walk

Plan a walk with your child to search for signs of summer. Before you leave, have your child help you make a list of things you might see during the summer. Take the list with you when you go on your walk. Let your child put a check by the things you see.

The Fan Club

Fans are a great way to cool off in the summer heat. Show your child how to fold a sheet of paper back and forth to make a fan. Make one for yourself, as well. Take turns fanning each other to stay cool.

Summer Pops

Let your child help you combine 1 can (6 ounces) frozen orange juice concentrate, 6 ounces water, 1 cup plain yogurt, and 1 teaspoon vanilla. Pour into popsicle molds. Freeze for several hours. Eat and enjoy.

Summer Song

Sung to: "Sing a Song of Sixpence"

Sing a song of sunshine,
Be happy every day.
Sing a song of sunshine,
You'll chase the clouds away.
Be happy every moment,
No matter what you do.
Just sing and sing and sing and sing,
And let the sun shine through!

Jean Warren

Bus, Bus

Bus, bus, may I have a ride?

Yes, yes, please step inside.

Put in some money.

Step on the gas.

Chug-a-way, chug-a-way,

But not too fast.

Take turns being the bus driver and the passenger as you recite this rhyme.

Adapted Traditional

I Went on Vacation

Play this alphabet memory game with your child. Start by saying, "I went on vacation and I rode in an automobile." Have your child follow with, "I went on vacation and I rode in an automobile and a bus." Take turns, each time adding a new vehicle whose name begins with the next letter of the alphabet. Continue as long as you can.

All Aboard!

Help your child arrange some chairs in a row to make a plane, train, bus, or other vehicle. Take turns pretending to be the passenger and the driver. Let her make tickets, maps, and other things she might need for travel.

Map Fun

Cover an old map with clear self-stick paper. Let your child use a dark crayon to trace some of the roads on the map. Let her select a starting point and an ending point for a vacation. Have her trace the roads to show how she would get from one to the other. Talk about the other symbols on the map.

Mini-Car Painting

Give your child a miniature car and a large sheet of paper. Pour some tempera paint into a shallow container. Have your child dip the wheels of the car in the paint and then "drive" it across the paper to leave paint tracks.

Egg Carton Train

Cut a row of six egg cups out of an egg carton, and cut a 2-inch section from a cardboard tube. Have your child glue the tube on top of the first egg cup to make the smokestack for the train. Let her paint her train as she wishes.

Travel Snack

Find a container or plate with dividers. Let your child help you prepare a snack, putting a different finger food in each section. Put on the lid or cover the plate with foil. Let your child take her Travel Snack on a pretend trip.

July

Fireworks in the Sky

Sung to: "Row, Row, Row Your Boat"

Boom, crack, whistle, pop,
Fireworks in the sky.
See them lighting up the night
On the Fourth of July.

Red, blue, gold, and green,
With fireworks we say,
"Happy Birthday, America,
It's Independence Day!"

Have your child pop up and down like fireworks while you sing this song.

Elizabeth McKinnon

Red, White, and Blue Shoes

Find an old pair of white tennis shoes for your child. Let your child decorate them with red and blue fabric paint. Encourage him to make Fourth of July designs such as stars, stripes, and fireworks.

Confetti Sparkler

Cover a cardboard paper towel tube with aluminum foil, leaving an extra 3 inches of foil at each end. Seal one end by folding up the extra foil. Have your child fill the tube with paper confetti. Loosely twist the foil at the open end to form a "wick." Let your child hold his Confetti Sparkler by the sealed end and wave it around to make the confetti fly.

Firecracker Dance

Save some plastic bubble wrap from a package (or ask a friend or a business if they have some). Have your child jump on the bubble wrap to burst the bubbles and make a lively popping sound. Be sure to join in for a few pops yourself!

Firework Art

Pour a small amount of white tempera paint into a shallow container. Set out a black sheet of construction paper and a paper towel. Show your child how to crumple the towel, dip it into the paint, and then gently press it onto the black paper. Have him notice how the print that is left looks like exploding fireworks. Repeat with other colors of paint as you wish.

Boom, Bang, Bang

Let your child collect a variety of metal pots and pans for drums. Have him arrange his "drum set" all around him. Give him wooden spoons for drumsticks. Play some patriotic music, such as "Stars and Stripes Forever." Let him beat along to the music. Encourage him to listen for changes in the music from fast to slow or from loud to soft, and to change his drumbeats to match.

Patriotic Snack

Cut circles out of bread and toast them. Let your child help you spread cream cheese on the toast circles. Help him arrange strawberry slices or blueberries in star shapes on top of the cream cheese.

Tube Town

Give your child cardboard tubes and tape. Let her create a town with the tubes by taping them together. Encourage her to add other props to her town as she wishes.

Tube Binoculars

Tape two toilet tissue tubes together to make binoculars. Add a yarn neck strap, if you wish. Let your child use her "binoculars" to observe birds and other outdoor creatures.

Racetrack Fun

Collect two long cardboard tubes like the kind giftwrap is rolled onto. Let your child help find two small toy cars that will fit inside the tubes. Prop the tubes against a chair and roll one car down the inside of each tube. Watch to see which car comes out first. Measure to see which car travels the farthest.

Designer Tube

Dip 12-inch lengths of thick yarn in white glue. Arrange the yarn around a cardboard tube. Allow the tube to dry overnight. Show your child how to carefully roll the Designer Tube in a shallow pan of paint then onto a sheet of paper to make a design. Let your child make as many Designer Tubes as she wishes.

Tube Wristbands

Cut 1- to 2-inch lengths from a cardboard tube. Let your child decorate the cardboard rings with felt tip markers or stickers. Cut each ring in one place. Show your child how to slide the rings around her wrists.

Snack Tube

Put a small snack in a plastic bag. Put the bag inside a cardboard tube. Wrap the tube in tissue paper or a paper napkin. Fasten the ends closed with ribbon. Let your child open her Snack Tube to discover her treat.

Wristband Hokey-Pokey

Sung to: "Hokey-Pokey"

You put your wristbands in,
You take your wristbands out.
You put your wristbands in,
And you shake them all about.
You do the Hokey-Pokey
And you turn yourself around.
That's what it's all about!

Have your child wear her wristbands and do the actions while you sing this song.

Adapted Traditional

July

A Trip to the Store

Take your child to a grocery store or produce stand to purchase a whole watermelon. Let him select the melon. Have him hold the melon and try to guess how much it weighs. Put it on the scale. Show him how to read the weight. How close was his guess? If the grocer sells precut melons, encourage your child to look at them. He may be surprised to learn that some watermelons are yellow on the inside.

Watermelon Painting

Give your child half of a white paper plate. Have him paint the rim of the plate green and the center red, pink, or yellow. When the paint has dried, let him glue real watermelon seeds to the plate.

Melon Checkup

Examine a whole watermelon with your child. Help him measure it with a measuring tape. Can he lift the melon? What kind of sound does it make when it is gently thumped? Ask your child to predict what might happen if he put the watermelon into water. Would it sink or float? Let your child test his prediction in the sink or bathtub. (The watermelon will float.)

Watermelon Juice

Have your child place several seedless watermelon chunks in a resealable plastic bag. Seal the bag. Let him squish and mash the watermelon chunks to make a thick "juice." Open up one end of the seal on the bag and stick in a straw. Let your child enjoy his homemade juice.

Sweet Treat

Slice up some watermelon for a snack. If it has seeds, ask your child to save his for later activities. If possible, compare different varieties of watermelon. Does yellow watermelon taste different from the red variety? Is "seedless" watermelon really seedless?

Watermelon Cutup

Let your child watch as you cut up a watermelon. Talk about half and quarter. Cut the watermelon in half. Cut those halves in half. Cut each of those halves in quarters, and so on. Then enjoy a piece of watermelon together.

Many Seeds

Sung to: "Frère Jacques"

I see one seed,

I see two seeds,

I see three,

I see four.

Watermelon has

A lot of little seeds—

Are there more?

Are there more?

Marjorie Debowy

Twinkle, Twinkle

Sung to: "Twinkle, Twinkle, Little Star"

Twinkle, twinkle, little stars,
Friends of Jupiter and Mars.
All you do the whole night long
Is twinkle while I sing my song.
Twinkle, twinkle, little stars,
Friends of Jupiter and Mars.

Jean Warren

Star Chart

Make a chart with seven squares. Help your child choose a chore or activity to do. Each time she does that activity, let her put a star in one of the squares. When all of the squares have stars, let her pick out a treat.

Star Scope

Tape a black construction paper circle to the bottom of a cardboard tube. Show your child how to carefully use a toothpick to poke holes in the paper-covered end of her tube. Encourage your child to make a design or pattern with the holes. To use her scope, have her hold it up to the light and look through the uncovered end. The light will shine through the holes, creating a miniature planetarium.

Design a Constellation

Talk about how the stars in the sky outline different shapes. If you can, point out the Big Dipper in the night sky. Give your child a sheet of paper and some self-stick stars. Let her arrange the stars on the paper to make her own constellation. Have her connect the stars to show the shape. Encourage her to write the name of her constellation at the top of her paper.

Math Stars

Cut star shapes out of heavy paper. On each point of the star, write half of a simple math equation that your child knows, such as 1+1. Write the answer to each equation on a spring-type clothespin. Give your child the star and the clothespins. Have her read the equation, say the answer, and clip the clothespin with the correct answer onto that point of the star.

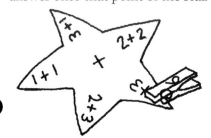

Wish Upon a Star

Cut a star shape out of cardboard. Let your child cover it with aluminum foil. Tell her it is a special wishing star: Whoever is holding the star gets to make a wish. Let her make a wish before giving the star to you to make a wish.

Star Cookies

Roll out refrigerated sugar cookie dough or prepare your favorite recipe. Let your child help you cut the dough into star shapes. Put the stars on a baking sheet and have your child sprinkle on colored sugar crystals before baking. Eat while you enjoy a night looking at the stars.

August

We Love It So

Sung to: "The Farmer in the Dell"

A-camping we will go,

A-camping we will go.

Heigh-ho, we love it so,

A-camping we will go.

Jean Warren

Backyard Campsite

Help your child set up a backyard camping area. Let him help you set up a tent, if you have one, or string up a tarp or blanket between two trees or posts. Give him blankets, a flashlight, and other camping gear. Then let him explore the adventures of "camping."

Nature Hike

Go on a Nature Hike with your child. Give him an egg carton for collecting treasures. Take along binoculars and a magnifying glass, if you have them. Encourage your child to look for signs of animals and to compare the different plants and animals he sees.

Campsite Art

Fold a rectangle of cardboard in half crosswise to form a tent shape. Have your child glue the objects he found on your Nature Hike onto the tent shape to create a collage. Let him find additional objects to add to his collage, if he would like.

Follow My Trail

Make a trail for your child to follow. Arrange rocks on the ground in the shape of arrows to show him which way to go. Have a small surprise waiting for him at the end of the trail. Let him help you make another trail for someone else.

Flashlight Hike

At dusk, gather some flashlights and lead your child on a short walk outdoors. Shine your flashlight on trees, up at the sky, on the ground, and so on. Do you see any animals? The next day, go on a flashlight hike indoors.

Trail Mix

Give your child a resealable plastic bag. Help him fill it with small scoops of a variety of finger foods such as dried cereal, raisins, peanuts, dried fruit, and small crackers. Have him seal his bag and shake to mix it all up. Let him enjoy his Trail Mix sitting outside in his "tent."

Concentration Pool

Collect an even number of opaque plastic lids. Divide the lids into pairs. Use a waterproof marker to draw the exact same picture, word, or number on each pair. Let your child put the lids face down in a wading pool filled with water. Have her turn over two lids at a time to find the ones that match.

Sprinkler Fun

Set up a sprinkler so that it sprays into the pool. Your child will love the refreshing drops of cool water. If you wish, give her an umbrella to use in the pool to keep out of the "rain."

Deep-Sea Numbers

Large metal washers make wonderful "treasures." Purchase a supply at your local hardware store. (The 2-inch ones are perfect.) Use a permanent marker to mark each one with a different math problem such as $2+3=\_\_$. Scatter the washers on the bottom of your wading pool. Let your child reach into the water, take one out, and solve the problem on it. Continue until all of the washers have been taken out.

Sink or Float?

Let your child help you collect a variety of objects from around your home. Have her take the objects out to the pool. One by one, have her select an object, predict whether it will sink or float, then test her hypothesis. Did she guess correctly? Let her separate the objects into two piles: sinkers and floaters.

Washcloth Experiment

Give your child several washcloths. Have her get the washcloths wet in the pool and wring out the extra water. Help her choose different spots to hang the washcloths up to dry. As the day goes on, have her check the washcloths. Does a washcloth dry faster in the shade or in the sun? Outside or inside?

Poolside Punch

Let your child help you make this sparkly drink. Mix 2 cups fruit-flavored juice drink with 1 cup club soda. Stir gently to combine. Serve over ice in plastic cups. Enjoy while sitting at your pool.

Water, Water

Sung to: "Twinkle, Twinkle, Little Star"

Water, water everywhere,

On my face and on my hair.

On my fingers, on my toes,

Water, water on my nose.

Water, water everywhere,

On my face and on my hair.

Jean Warren

August

Fossil Hunt

Bury several plastic dinosaurs in your sandbox or in a large pan of sand. Let your child go on a "fossil hunt" using a spoon to search in the sandbox for dinosaurs. When he discovers a dinosaur, ask him to name it by looking carefully at its characteristics.

Fossil Prints

Knead a handful of modeling dough until it is soft and elastic. Show your child how to make "fossils" by pressing one of his small plastic dinosaurs into the dough and then carefully removing it to reveal the imprint left behind. Let him make a fossil from each of his dinosaurs.

Dinosaur Fact Book

Staple several sheets of construction paper together. Help your child write a different dinosaur fact on each page, such as "Dinosaurs lived a long time ago. Many dinosaurs were huge. Some dinosaurs ate leaves." Let him illustrate each page to complete it.

Prehistoric Parade

Play selections of instrumental music with different beats. Listen to the music with your child. Think of a dinosaur it reminds you of, and move around the room while you pretend to be that kind of dinosaur. For example, a march might remind you of a tyrannosaurus, slow music an apatosaurus, and so on.

Tyrannosaurus Toss

Draw a picture of a large tyrannosaurus head on a piece of sturdy cardboard. Use a sharp knife to cut out the dinosaur's mouth, including several large teeth. Prop the piece of cardboard against a chair. Give your child some beanbags and let him "feed the dinosaur" by tossing the beanbags into its mouth.

Dinosaur Delights

Let your child help you prepare a snack or a meal that includes meat for a meat-eating dinosaur and vegetables for a veggie-eating dinosaur. Let him pretend to be a ferocious meat eater and a gentle plant eater while eating each kind of food.

All Around the Swamp

Sung to: "The Wheels on the Bus"

The pteranodon's wings went

Flap, flap, flap,

Flap, flap, flap,

Flap, flap, flap.

The pteranodon's wings went

Flap, flap, flap,

All around the swamp.

Yosie Yoshimura

Stamp Your Card

Sung to: "Row, Row, Row Your Boat"

Stamp, stamp, stamp your card,

Stamp it all around.

Now count the stamps that you have made.

How many have you found?

Let your child make rubber stamp prints on an index card while you sing this song. Then have her count the number of prints she made.

Ellen Bedford

Fancy Placemats

Let your child make placemats for your family. Give her sheets of construction paper and some rubber stamps and an ink pad. Let her stamp designs all over the construction paper. Encourage her to try making patterns with the designs.

Gift Note Pads

Let your child help you collect unmarked scrap paper you have saved for recycling. Cut the paper into the desired size and staple them together to make a note pad. Have your child stamp a different design at the bottom of each page. Let her keep the note pad for herself or give it away as a gift.

Silly Story

Put five rubber stamps that are of familiar shapes into a bag. Have your child begin telling a story by taking a rubber stamp from the bag, stamping the design on a sheet of paper, and making up a sentence about it. Write down the sentence as she speaks. Let her continue with the remaining stamps. When they all have been used, read the story back to your child.

Hidden Picture Game

Cover a piece of light-colored construction paper with prints made from an assortment of rubber stamps. Choose an additional rubber stamp, such as one in the shape of a kitten. Somewhere among the prints on the paper, stamp one kitten print. Give the paper to your child and ask her to "find the kitty."

Rubber Stamp Tic-Tac-Toe

Draw a tic-tac-toe grid on a sheet of paper. Collect two different rubber stamps and an ink pad. Invite your child to join you for a game of tic-tac-toe. Instead of marking *X*'s and *O*'s, make prints with your different rubber stamps. The first person to have three stamps in a row or diagonally wins.

Snack Invitation

Fold a sheet of paper in half to make a card, and make some rubber stamp designs on the front. On the inside of the card write out an invitation, asking your child to join you for a snack today. Deliver it to her and help her read it. Then sit down and enjoy a snack together. If you wish, let your child make invitations to deliver to other family members or a friend or two.

September

Off to School

Sung to: "The Farmer in the Dell"

Off to school we go,

It's off to school we go.

We'll learn our ABC's

And more

With everyone we know.

Judy Hall

This Is the Way

Follow the path your child will take to school. If he will be walking, walk along the route he'll take each day. If he will be riding a bus, call the school to find out the bus route and drive along it. If you'll be driving him, hop in the car and drive to him school. Talk about the things you see along the way.

My Own Room

Once you are at the school, take time to explore. If possible, show your child his classroom. Walk around the school, looking for the library, cafeteria, gym, and other places. Play on the playground. Spending time at the school together will help your child feel more comfortable when he is there on his own.

Time for School

Find a clock with a face and hands you can adjust. Change the time on the clock to show your child the times he will start and finish school. Let him move the hands to the two times and tell you if it's time to start school or time to finish school and go home.

After-School Snack

Prepare a special treat to share after school with your child. You could fix his favorite food or have a special ready-made treat for him. Encourage him to talk about his day as you share the snack together. Ask him directed questions such as "What did you do at recess? Where did you sit? What songs did you sing?" instead of yes-or-no questions.

Pocketful of Love

If your child seems a little nervous about going to school, give him a Pocketful of Love to take along. Pretend to put lots of kisses in your hands and carefully place the "kisses" in one of your child's pockets. (If your child's clothing has no pockets, put the kisses inside a shirt, in a shoe, or behind an ear.) Whenever your child is worried, tell him to reach into his pocket and pull out one of the kisses.

School Supplies

Let your child go with you when you shop for school supplies. Help him make out a list of what he will need. At the store, let him find items from the list and cross them off.

A Library Visit

Plan a time to take your child to the library. At many libraries, if a child can write her name, she is old enough to get her own library card. When she can get her own library card, let her carry it in a special pocket or backpack and use it to check out her own library materials.

Library Treasure Hunt

Before you go to the library, make a list of some items for your child to look for while you are there. For example, your list could include a globe, videos, music CDs, encyclopedias, artwork, and a water fountain. Walk around the library with your child, looking for all the items on your list. Can she find any more special things?

Book Limit

Set a limit on the number of books your child may check out, perhaps six or seven. Have your child place the books she is interested in on a table. Help your child count out her favorite books. Have your child stack the books from largest to smallest and then carry them to the checkout counter.

Ask the Librarian

Have your child think of a special kind of book she would like to read. It could be a book with a favorite character, or one about a special topic. Let your child ask the librarian to help her find the book on the library shelf.

Pictures Make the Story

Let your child select a picture book with interesting illustrations. Sit down with your child and "read" the book together by just looking at the pictures and describing what is happening in them. Help your child notice various details in the pictures that give clues to the story. Next, tell the story again, this time reading the words. Compare the two stories. Did the pictures tell all of the story? Which story did your child prefer?

Library Trip Snack

Pack a simple snack to enjoy with your child after your trip to the library. Eat your snack outside the library or at a nearby park.

The Library

Sung to: "Twinkle, Twinkle, Little Star"

The library is the place for me.

It has lots of books, you see.

I check them out, one by one,

And return them when I'm done.

The library is the place for me.

It has lots of books, you see.

Have your child stack up her library books as you sing this song.

Gayle Bittinger

September

Fall Picnic

Pack up a picnic with some fall treats such as apple slices, apple cider, and pumpkin bread. Take your picnic outside to eat. Look all around with your child to find a place to sit where you can observe fall activities together. You could sit by a tree that is losing its leaves or find a place to watch a squirrel getting ready for winter.

Fall Mosaic

Let your child help you collect assorted dried beans and peas, pasta pieces, and popcorn kernels. Have him spread a thick layer of glue on the inside of a plastic lid. Let him arrange the collected items on the glue to make a mosaic picture.

Fall Hike

Go on a nature hike with your child and look for signs of fall. What animals do you see? What are they doing? Have your child look carefully at the trees. What is happening to them? Are any flowers still blooming? Take along a paper sack and let your child collect a few signs of fall to bring home.

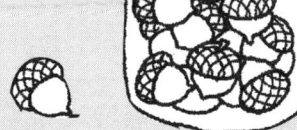

Leaf Creatures

Let your child select two or three leaves from your nature hike. Have him glue the leaves onto construction paper. Show him how to use felt tip markers to add details, such as arms, legs, faces, and hats, to the leaves to turn them into creatures. Encourage him to make a Leaf Creature family.

Estimating Game

Fill a jar partway with a fall item such as leaves or acorns. Have your child guess how many are in the jar. Take the items out and count them together. Was his guess too high or too low? Play the game as many times as you like, putting in a different number of items each time.

Fall Delight

Peel and thinly slice a baking apple. Let your child put half of the slices in one small bowl and the other half in another bowl. Dab on a little butter. Have your child sprinkle on brown sugar and cinnamon. Cook the apples in the microwave for 1 or 2 minutes, or until the apples are soft. Cool and enjoy.

Fall Leaves

Sung to: "Row, Row, Row Your Boat"

Down, down, yellow and brown,

The leaves fall to the ground.

Rake them up in a pile so high

Until they reach the sky.

Pretend to rake leaves as you sing.

Adapted Traditional

Jumping Song

Sung to: "Skip to My Lou"

Jump, jump side to side,

Jump, jump side to side,

Jump, jump side to side,

Jump the rope, my darling.

Have your child jump side to side while you sing.

Gayle Bittinger

Jump With Me

Help your child learn or practice jump rope skills by stretching a jump rope out on the ground. Show her how to keep her feet together and jump from side to side over the rope. Sing the "Jumping Song" while she jumps.

Circle Jump

Lay a jump rope on the ground in a circle shape. When you say "In," have your child jump into the circle. When you say "Out," have her jump out of the circle. Ask her to listen carefully because sometimes you might say "In" or "Out" two times in a row.

Spin and Jump

Stand in middle of a large space and hold one end of a jump rope. Spin around so that the rope goes around you like the hands on a clock. Have your child stand in one spot and jump over the rope whenever it spins by her.

Dice Toss

Collect one or two dice. Let your child throw the dice and count the dots that turn up. Have her jump over her jump rope that many times.

Jumping Practice

Without a jump rope at first, let your child practice jumping slowly and quickly. Have her listen as you name something that moves. If it is something that moves slowly, such as a turtle or a tractor, have her jump slowly. If it is something that moves quickly, such as a rabbit or a racecar, have her jump quickly.

Roped-Up Snack

Buy some licorice ropes. Put some finger food, such as cereal or raisins, in a small plastic bag. Wrap a licorice rope around the bag and tie it in a bow. Let your child untie the licorice and enjoy it with her snack.

October

More Pieces

Sung to: "Did You Ever See a Lassie"

The more I look around,

Around, around;

The more I look around,

More pieces are found.

First one piece,

Then two,

Then three,

Then four.

The more I look around,

More pieces are found.

Sing while your child is looking for puzzle pieces in the Treasure Puzzle activity.

Jean Warren

Puzzle Piece Frame

Save puzzles with missing pieces to make puzzle art. Let your child select a variety of interesting puzzle pieces. Have him paint the pieces all one color or a variety of colors. Find an old picture frame. Help your child glue the painted puzzle pieces all around the frame to make a new, colorful frame.

Puzzle Mix-Up

Collect two or three simple, familiar puzzles. Mix up the puzzle pieces and spread them out on a table. Let your child try to sort out the pieces and put the different puzzles together.

Photo Puzzle

Have a favorite family photo enlarged to a 5-by-7-inch or 8-by-10-inch size. Mount the photo on heavy paper. Cut the photo into puzzle pieces and put them in an envelope. Let your child put the puzzle together to discover his very own family.

Puzzle Letter

Write your child a letter on sturdy paper. Cut the letter into several puzzle pieces. Give the pieces to your child to put together. What does the letter say? If you wish, have your child create Puzzle Letters of his own by writing a letter to a friend or family member on sturdy paper, cutting it into puzzle pieces, and sending it off to the recipient.

Treasure Puzzle

Hide a small treasure in a special place. Draw a simple picture of this place on a sheet of sturdy paper. Cut the paper into puzzle pieces. Hide the pieces all around a room. Have your child find the pieces, put the puzzle together, and discover the location of the hidden treasure. Sing "More Pieces" while your child hunts for puzzle pieces.

Sandwich Puzzle

Make a peanut butter sandwich for your child. Cut the sandwich into several puzzle pieces. Let your child put his sandwich together before eating it.

Pizza Collage

Give your child a large circle cut out of heavy paper. Have her color on red "sauce." Set out scraps of various colors of construction paper and let her cut out any toppings she might want to put on her pizza. For example, she could cut thin strips of white and yellow paper for cheese, brown mushrooms, brown sausage, yellow pineapple, and so on. Let her glue her toppings on her pizza.

Pizza Fractions

Cut three large circles out of heavy paper. Cut one circle into halves, one into quarters, and one into eighths. Help your child discover different ways to create whole pizzas by putting one half, two quarters, and four eighths together or three quarters and two eighths together. How many combinations can she find?

Favorite Toppings

Help your child write the names of several different pizza toppings on a sheet of paper. Have her interview family members and friends, asking them what toppings they like. Have her put a check by a topping each time it is named. When she is finished interviewing people, help her look at the results. Which topping was the most popular? Which one was the least popular?

Pizza Wheelin'

Give your child some modeling dough, a pizza pan, a rolling pin, and a pizza cutter. Let her have fun rolling out the dough, putting it in the pan, and cutting it with the pizza cutter.

Pizza Delivery

Play a Pizza Delivery game with your child. Pretend to call her up on the phone and order a pizza. Have her "make" the pizza and deliver it to you. (You could even use the modeling dough pizza from the Pizza Wheelin' activity.) Then trade places so your child orders a pizza and you deliver it to her.

Pizza Crackers

Have your child arrange about a dozen sturdy crackers on a baking sheet. Help her spoon a little tomato sauce or pizza sauce on top of each cracker. Let her sprinkle some grated mozzarella cheese on top of the sauce. Broil until cheese is melted. Allow Pizza Crackers to cool before eating.

Pizza Treat

Sung to: "Twinkle, Twinkle, Little Star"

It is round and made of dough,

Topped with cheese and sauce just so.

It's a big, round, tasty treat

Filled with vegetables and meat.

It's a pizza cooked just right.

Are you ready? Have a bite!

Pretend to make a pizza while you sing this song.

Diane Thom

October

All About Bats

Find a book about bats so you and your child can learn some interesting facts about them. Bats are the only mammals that can fly (bats are not birds). Bats' wings are also their arms. Bats hang upside down to rest. Most bats are timid and harmless to people. Help your child discover even more about these amazing creatures.

Clip-On Bats

Draw small bat wing shapes on black construction paper. Help your child cut out the shapes. Have him glue the shapes to clothespins you have painted black. Let him clip the bats all around your home.

Bat Sounds

Bats rely on their keen hearing to locate objects in the dark. Have your child pretend to be a bat and close his eyes. Quietly move to a different location in the room. Make a soft sound and have your child listen carefully and point to where he thinks the sound is coming from. Switch places and play the game again.

Bug Hunt

Some bats eat fruit and others eat insects. Insect-eating bats are very helpful to farmers because they eat insects that eat their crops. Pretend to be a bat along with your child and go outside on an insect hunt. How many bugs can you find?

Fly Like a Bat

Find a piece of black fabric or a black scarf. Use safety pins to attach the fabric to the cuffs and collar of your child's shirt. Let your child "fly" around the room flapping his bat wings. When he wants to stop, have him lie down by a chair and put his feet on it (to look like he's hanging upside down).

Bat Snack

Some bats live on a diet of fruit. Let your child help you pick one or two fruits to prepare and enjoy for a snack.

The Bats Fly By

Sung to: "The Farmer in the Dell"

The bats fly by at night.

The bats fly by at night.

They dive and soar,

I see some more.

The bats are quite a sight.

Pretend to watch bats soaring by as you sing this song.

Gayle Bittinger

Trick or Treat

Sung to: "Frère Jacques"

Trick or treat,

Trick or treat,

Halloween night,

Halloween night.

In our costumes playing,

You will hear us saying,

"Trick or treat,

Trick or treat."

Pretend to trick or treat while you sing this song.

Gayle Bittinger

Permanent Pumpkins

Bring in several large smooth stones with rounded shapes to use for making "pumpkins." Let your child paint the stones orange. Allow the paint to dry. Have your child cut green construction paper stems to attach to the top of each stone pumpkin. Display the Permanent Pumpkins on a porch or beside a doorway.

Trick or Treat Container

Cut the top off a plastic gallon milk jug, leaving the handle intact. Help your child cut eye, nose, mouth, and ear shapes out of various colors of construction paper. Let her glue them to the jug. Give her pieces of yarn to glue around the opening to make "hair."

What's Missing?

Place six or seven Halloween objects on a table. Have your child look at them and then close her eyes. Take away one of the objects. Ask your child to open her eyes and tell you which object is missing. Make the game harder by taking away more than one object. Switch places and let your child take away objects while you guess.

Hanging Spiders

Have your child paint both sides of several paper plates black. When the paint is dry, have her cut thin strips of black paper for spider legs. Let her glue eight paper legs and two wiggly eyes on each spider. Attach a piece of yarn to the center of each plate and hang it from the ceiling or a doorway.

Jack-O'-Lantern Face

Give your child a handful of orange modeling dough to press into a round lid from a plastic container. Give her some popcorn kernels to arrange on the dough to make a jack-o'-lantern face.

Mystery Juice

Use water tinted with red food coloring to make ice cubes. Let your child help you make lemonade. Pour two glasses of lemonade and put one or two ice cubes in each glass. As you stir your icy drink, have your child notice what is happening to the color of the lemonade.

November

Crack a Shell

Sung to: "The Mulberry Bush"

If you want to crack a shell,

Crack a shell, crack a shell,

If you want to crack a shell,

Use a nutcracker.

Substitute the names of other things you can use to crack a nutshell for *nutcracker.*

Gayle Bittinger

Nutcracker

Show your child several different kinds of unshelled nuts. Ask him to think of ways to crack open the nuts to get to the meat inside. Discuss possible solutions such as pounding the shells with a rock or stepping on them. Let your child try out his ideas.

Nutshell Collage

Save the shells from a variety of nuts you and your child have cracked. Break them into pieces of different sizes. Let your child arrange and glue the nutshells on a square of cardboard to make a collage.

Nut Transfer

Set out unshelled nuts, an ice cube tray, and a pair of small kitchen tongs. Let your child use the tongs to place one nut in each compartment of the ice cube tray.

Counting Game

Put out a bowl of unshelled nuts and a large die. Let your child roll the die and call out the number that comes up. Have him take that many nuts from the bowl and put them in front of him. Take turns rolling the die and taking nuts from the bowl until all the nuts are gone. Whoever has the most nuts at the end of the game wins.

Walnut Shell Racing

Use a smooth board make a ramp. Set out two walnut shell halves and two marbles. Give your child one of the walnut shell halves and a marble. Show him how to put the shell upside down over the marble at the top of the ramp. Have him let go and watch his shell race down the ramp. Put your shell and marble at the top of the ramp at the same time and race your child's shell to the "finish line."

Nut Tasting

Chop up two or three different kinds of nuts. Give your child a banana to dip into plain or vanilla yogurt, then into one of the kinds of chopped nuts. Let him taste each kind of nut. Which one does he like best?

Build a Bridge

Help your child turn an empty shoebox into a bridge for toy cars. Turn the box upside down and cut open the corner seams at both ends to create ramps for cars to drive over. Trim the two long sides and cut semicircles, as shown. Have your child use felt tip markers or crayons to decorate the outside of the bridge.

Block Bridge

Show your child how to make more bridges by combining blocks and pieces of cardboard. Have her build up columns of equal height with blocks. Give her a long piece of cardboard to put across the columns. Let her make as many bridges as she would like.

Sink Bridge

Span your sink with this simple bridge. Find a piece of vinyl (a discarded tablecloth or shower curtain works well). Cut a 5-inch-wide strip of vinyl that is about 8 inches longer than your sink. Stretch the vinyl strip from one side of the sink to the other, taping it in place with duct tape. Fill the sink partway with water. Your child will love helping plastic action figures and animals cross the bridge and dive into the water.

Bridge to Eat

Let your child snack on this tasty bridge. Give her four thin pretzel sticks and four jumbo marshmallows. Have her poke a pretzel stick into each marshmallow and connect the marshmallows to form bridge supports. Give her one whole graham cracker to rest on top of the marshmallows.

Suspension Bridge

Draw the outline of a suspension bridge on a large sheet of paper. Give your child an ink pad or make a paint pad by pouring a small amount of paint on a folded paper towel in a shallow container. Have your child press her fingertips onto the ink pad and then onto the bridge outline to make a colorful bridge. When the ink is dry, put the bridge on the floor where your child can drive small cars and other vehicles across it.

Bridge Walk

Find a footbridge in your area and take your child on a walk across it. Together, look at how the bridge was built. What materials were used? What does the bridge go over? As you travel around town, encourage your child to keep her eyes open for any kind of bridge. How many can she find?

Over the Bridge

Sung to: "The Bear Went Over the Mountain"

The bridge goes over the water,

The bridge goes over the water.

The bridge goes over the water,

And I go over the bridge.

Substitute the names of other things a bridge might go over, such as a road or railroad tracks, for *water*.

Susan Hodges

November

Vegetable Stew

Draw a bowl shape on construction paper and have your child cut it out. Talk about what a stew is with your child. Have him glue his construction paper bowl to a sheet of construction paper. Then let him cut pictures of vegetables from magazines and vegetable can labels and glue the pictures on top of his bowl shape. Have him name all the vegetables in his bowl of "stew."

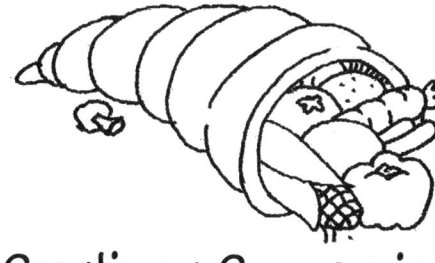

Creating a Cornucopia

Take your child to the store to purchase a variety of fresh vegetables he likes or would like to try. Bring the vegetables home and let your child arrange them in a cornucopia or other basket. Encourage your child to describe the different colors, patterns, sizes, and weights of the vegetables.

Which Vegetable?

Have your child look at the vegetables in the cornucopia. Ask him to listen carefully while you describe a vegetable, then ask him to guess which one you are talking about. Let him have a turn describing a vegetable for you to guess.

Vegetable Patterns

Collect several of two or three kinds of vegetables, such as potatoes, carrots, and mushrooms. Encourage your child to arrange the vegetables on the kitchen counter in a pattern. For example, potato-potato-carrot-potato-potato-carrot or mushroom-carrot-potato-mushroom-carrot-potato.

Harvest Stew

Use the vegetables from your cornucopia to make stew. Put 1 cup of tomato juice in a crock pot and turn the crock pot on high. Let your child help you prepare the vegetables for the stew. Allow the stew to cook for 1 to 2 hours. Cool and eat.

Sharing With Nature

Save the vegetable peelings and scraps from the Harvest Stew. Cut a grapefruit in half and remove the fruit to make two bowls. Cut the fruit into small pieces. Have your child mix the vegetable peelings and scraps with the fruit. Then let him fill the grapefruit bowls with the mixture and place them outside for birds and other animals. Have your child observe the bowls each day to see how they have changed.

Lots of Stew

Sung to: "The Farmer in the Dell"

There's lots of stew for me,

There's lots of stew for you.

There's plenty of stew

For a hungry few.

There's stew for me and you.

Susan M. Paprocki

Thanksgiving Time

Sung to: "The Farmer in the Dell"

Thanksgiving time is here.

Let's give a great big cheer

For food and friends and family.

Thanksgiving time is here.

Gayle Bittinger

Place Cards

Let your child make place cards for your Thanksgiving table. Help your child cut construction paper into 4-inch squares, one for each person coming for dinner. Show her how to fold each square in half. Help her write each person's name on one of the folded squares. Give her holiday stickers to put on the place cards. Let her set the place cards around the table.

Cranberry Relish

Let your child help you use a food grinder to grind up one 12-ounce bag of fresh cranberries, 1 unpeeled orange cut into wedges, and ¹/₂ cup walnut halves. Have her stir the ground mixture together and add sugar to taste. Serve alone or with turkey slices.

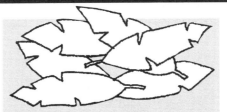

Thankful Feathers

Let your child help you cut feather shapes out of different colors of construction paper. Put the feathers in a paper bag. Have your child reach in and take out one of the feathers. Have her name something she is thankful for that is the same color as the feather. Take turns pulling out feathers until they are all out.

Turkey Hand Puppet

Help your child trace around her hand on a piece of light brown construction paper. Let her cut out her hand shape. Have her use crayons or felt tip markers to color the fingers on her hand shape as though they were feathers. Then have her draw a turkey face on the thumb. Attach a craft stick handle to complete the puppet. Have your child make more than one puppet, and put on a Thanksgiving puppet show for you.

Stuff the Turkey

Make a "turkey" by opening a large brown grocery sack and rolling down the top edges three or four times. Place the bag on the floor, open end up. Give your child 6-inch squares of newspaper. Have her "stuff the turkey" by crumpling the newspaper squares and tossing them inside the bag.

Thanksgiving Centerpieces

Give your child a 6-inch cardboard circle and a cardboard toilet tissue tube. Have your child cover the tube with glue and roll it in glitter. Help her glue the tube upright in the center of the cardboard circle. Let her glue small pine cones, acorn cups, and other assorted nature items around the base of her centerpiece. Give her a few dried flowers to place in the tube. Let her display her centerpiece on your Thanksgiving table.

December

Decorate

Sung to: "Three Blind Mice"

Decorate.

Decorate.

Frosting now.

Frosting now.

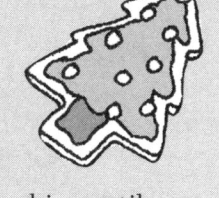

We bake the cookies until
they're done,

Now it's time to have some fun.

We'll decorate each and every
one.

Yum, yum, yum.

Pretend to decorate as you sing this
song.

Gayle Bittinger

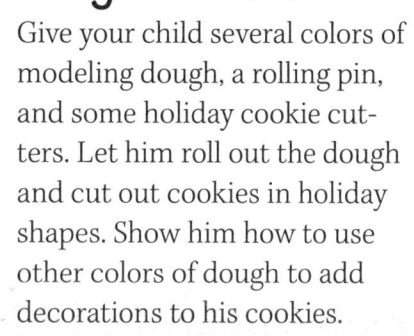

Paper Cookie Decorations

Trace around large holiday cookie
cutters on brown grocery sacks.
Help your child cut out the shapes
to make "cookies." Fill plastic
squeeze bottles with a runny mixture of flour and water. Add drops
of different food coloring to each
bottle. Set out the brown paper
cookie shapes. Let your child
"frost" the cookies by squeezing
on the colored flour and water
mixtures.

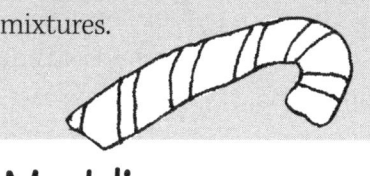

Modeling Dough Cookies

Give your child several colors of
modeling dough, a rolling pin,
and some holiday cookie cutters. Let him roll out the dough
and cut out cookies in holiday
shapes. Show him how to use
other colors of dough to add
decorations to his cookies.

Cookie Cutter Ornaments

Purchase a few inexpensive
metal holiday cookie cutters. Let
your child glue shiny decorations,
such as glitter, sequins, buttons,
and ribbon, all over the cookie
cutters. Help him tie a ribbon to
the top of each cookie cutter to
make a hanging decoration.

Cookie Matchups

On a sheet of heavy paper, trace
around three or four different
holiday cookie cutters with a felt
tip marker. Put the cookie cutters
in a paper bag. Have your child
pick a shape on the paper, then
reach into the bag to try to find
the matching cookie cutter, using
only his sense of touch.

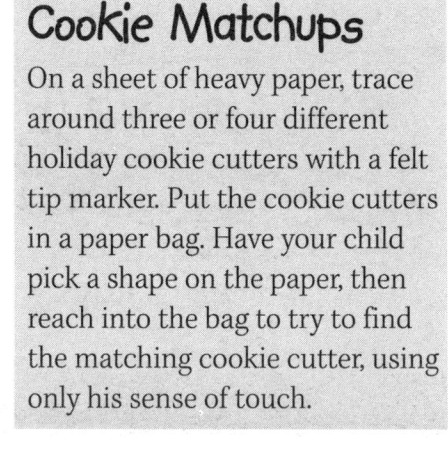

Simple Cookies I

Purchase ready-made sugar
cookie dough in your grocer's
refrigerator section. Let your
child help you roll out the dough
and cut it into holiday cookie
shapes. Bake the cookies according to the package directions.
Allow the cookies to cool. Let
your child spread on frosting
and add holiday sprinkles and
candy decorations.

Simple Cookies II

Purchase ready-made cookies in
holiday shapes. Let your child
spread on frosting and add
sprinkles and other holiday
candy decorations.

Giant Ornament

Cut a large round ornament shape out of construction paper. Cut old holiday cards or gift-wrap into small pieces. Have your child squeeze stripes of glue across her ornament shape. Have her place the small pieces of cards or gift-wrap on top of the glue. Hang it from the ceiling or in a window.

Plastic Foam Ornaments

Let your child help you press cookie cutters into plastic-foam food trays to cut out holiday shapes. Let your child decorate both sides of the shapes by brushing on glue and sprinkling on glitter. When the glue has dried, punch holes in the top of the shapes and insert yarn loops to make hangers.

Photo Ornament

Cut two identical holiday shapes out of wallpaper or posterboard. Cut a hole in the center of one of the shapes to make a picture frame. Have your child decorate both shapes with felt tip markers. Attach a photo of your child to the back of the shape with a hole in it, so the photo shows through. Glue the back of the second shape to the back of the picture frame. Punch a hole at the top and tie on yarn for a hanger.

Ornament Game

Let your child help you decorate your home or a tree with ornaments. Set out the ornaments you will be using. Give your child directions such as these: "Put the red ball up high. Put the silver bell next to the blue star. Put the green horn near the bottom." Continue until all the ornaments have been used.

I Spy

Whenever you have a collection of ornaments to look at, play I Spy with your child. Start by saying "I spy with my little eye an ornament that is blue." Have your child try to guess which ornament you are spying. Give her additional clues as needed until she guesses.

Ornament Bagels

Cut a bagel in half. Let your child help you spread cream cheese on both halves. Have diced red and green peppers and shredded carrots ready. Let your child use the vegetables to decorate her Ornament Bagels.

Hang the Ornaments

Sung to: "Twinkle, Twinkle, Little Star"

Hang the ornaments one by one,

They'll look pretty when we're done.

The ornaments are a pretty sight.

They shine and sparkle and look so bright.

Hang the ornaments one by one,

They'll look pretty when we're done.

Sing this song while your child hangs up real or pretend ornaments around the room.

Gayle Bittinger

December

Candle Display

Let your child help you find as many candles as possible. Help him arrange the candles on a table, placing candles on plates, trays, or other non-flammable surfaces. While he sits in a safe place and watches, light all of the candles and turn off the room lights. Sit together and enjoy the light from the candles. If you wish, tell or read a favorite holiday story in the candlelight.

Candle Puppet

Give your child a cardboard toilet tissue tube. Help him cover it with holiday stickers or holiday wrap. Have your child cut out a yellow flame shape and glue it to one end of a craft stick. Show him how to "light" his candle puppet by pushing the craft stick up through the cardboard tube.

How Many Candles?

Place a number of small candles (such as birthday candles) in a clear-plastic jar. Have your child look at the candles and try to guess how many are in the jar. Let him take out the candles and count them. Was his guess too high, too low, or just right? Repeat with a different number of candles.

Candle Printing

Make a paint pad by pouring a small amount of paint on a folded paper towel in a shallow container. Let your child select one or two candles. Show him how to press the ends of the candles on the paint pad and then onto a sheet of paper. Encourage him to make designs and patterns. If you wish, have more than one color of paint pad available.

Candle Comparisons

Let your child help you collect five or six candles of various sizes, colors, and fragrances. Have him set them out on a table. Let him use the candles for the following games: lining up the candles from shortest to longest; grouping the candles by color; sniffing the candles and trying to identify their scents.

Celery Candles

Cut whole celery stalks into pieces of equal length. Give two pieces to your child. Help him spread peanut butter inside both celery pieces. Show him how to press the celery pieces together to form a "candle." Use a vegetable peeler to make a small carrot curl. Have your child place the carrot curl on the top of his candle for a flame.

Light the Candles

Sung to: "Frère Jacques"

Light the candles,

Light the candles,

Oh, so bright,

Oh, so bright.

It is time to celebrate.

It is time to celebrate.

I can't wait,

I can't wait.

Let your child pretend to light candles as you sing this song.

Susan A. Miller